To Lori and Neil –
Here's to fond memories – past and future
a wonderful place we have shared with you
Mom and Dad
Christmas 1990

YOSEMITE

A landscape of life

PHOTOGRAPHS
BY
JAY MATHER

TEXT
BY
DALE MAHARIDGE

YOSEMITE
ASSOCIATION

A PUBLICATION OF
THE YOSEMITE ASSOCIATION
& THE SACRAMENTO BEE

Some visitors find the best view of Yosemite is
from the top, at Glacier Point. High clouds tower
above Half Dome in the high country.

COVER: A visitor celebrates the grandeur of
Yosemite by taking a careful walk at Glacier Point.

PREVIOUS PAGE: Yosemite Falls in the winter.

OVERLEAF: For most, the first view of Yosemite
comes when they emerge from the forested
Merced River Canyon into Yosemite Valley and
face the towering mass of El Capitan rising more
than a vertical half mile.

Copyright 1990

The Sacramento Bee
2100 Q Street
Sacramento, Calif. 95852

The Yosemite Association
P.O. Box 545
Yosemite National Park, Calif. 95389

Library of Congress Cataloging-in-Publication Data
Mather, Jay, 1946—
Yosemite: A landscape of life / Photographs by Jay Mather;
Text by Dale Maharidge.

P.   Cm.

ISBN 0-939666-56-1: $14.95
1. Yosemite National Park (Calif.)
2. Yosemite National Park (Calif.)—Pictorial Works
3. Travelers—California—Yosemite National Park—Biography
I. Maharidge, Dale.
II. Title.

F868.Y6M36 1990
979.4'47—dc20 90-41607 CIP

Printed in USA. First printing September 1990.

This book celebrates a special place of
towering mountains and cliffs.
It is also about the people who visit it.
Some come for only a few hours.
Others can never leave.

YOSEMITE
A
landscape of life

In all seasons, men and women are
dwarfed by the scale of Yosemite's
granite walls and snowy mountainsides.
These Nordic skiers are out for a run at
Badger Pass.

INTRODUCTION

The park has developed into a laboratory in which we can measure our civilization.

I t's god-awful cold. Ten below at last count. At 10 below, the snow is squeaky and crisp under your cross-country skis.

At 10 below, you don't think of much except the snowy trail beneath the moonlit night. The thoughts that exist concern this country's frightening vastness, that you are but an insignificant speck on the face of this great arc of granite and snow sweeping off the western Sierra toward Yosemite Valley and beyond, almost two miles down into the mist of the low country of cities and people and problems.

But those are distant worlds.

Up here in Tuolumne Meadows, a dozen miles from the nearest roadhead, there are only four other people. We are visiting them as part of a story on Yosemite National Park, not on the park in terms of its rocks and trees, but more precisely, a special group of people—the visitors and residents.

The result is this book. It was born of an idea by photographer Jay Mather, who spent two years journeying here with his camera. His purpose was simple: in all the decades of Yosemite's existence, most pictures have celebrated its natural attributes; in so many images you would think humans had not ever set foot here. The reality is that photographers must work hard to keep people out of their frames. Jay worked to get them in.

People are part of Yosemite National Park. Not only do humans have a role here, the park has developed into a laboratory in which we can measure our civilization.

This trip is but a small part of trying to understand how a few people fit into the scheme of this laboratory. Each winter, some 200 people ski over the back of the frozen Sierra, climbing a dozen miles into steadily thinning air, braving avalanches and blinding snow. When they arrive, they find a little cabin provided for winter wayfarers.

Tonight, two sleeping ski packers share the cabin with us. It's midnight and the stove is stoked. We'd spent the evening at the home of Brent and Tory Finley, the rangers who live in this snowbound wilderness six months each season, in a cabin about a mile from this one.

OPPOSITE: A group of German Baptists from Pennsylvania watches climbers on El Capitan while on a tour of the park with friends from Fresno. Newcomers to Yosemite Valley are always looking up.

The Finleys find not only a source of income here, but most importantly, a cadence of life. Unlike most of modern civilization, they see, as writer Carlos Castaneda says, the space between the leaves. And then they know something.

Others are more literal. A trail register signed by those who have come before us in the cabin offers some insight.

"Got to trudge the long road back to diseased Western civilization," writes Bodie Jack, "after a few brief days of crystal sun, brilliant moon, soda springs water and some of the most blatantly insanely euphoric powder skiing under heaven."

Well said. As I sit here writing by the light of a candle lantern, next to the now-hot stove, I find salvation in a cup of steaming tea and begin the difficult job of explaining the meaning of this park, which is something different to each of the several hundred permanent residents and the annual pilgrimage of 3 million visitors, such as Bodie Jack.

All meaning is not to be found up in these isolated heights 9,000 feet above the sea. For most visitors, their first and only view of the park comes a mile below, when they arrive at the valley entrance, in the Merced Canyon forested with black oaks and ponderosa pines. When they round a bend, on go the brake lights with the sight of El Capitan, the grand captain of all cliffs, and all the other valley cliffs with their waterfalls.

Anyone who has been to this park remembers that first sight that inspires people from fabled lands.

"If this was Alaska, you'd have to fly hours or hike weeks to get into it," a friend from that state said as our car emerged from the Wawona, or "Whiskey" Tunnel, so-dubbed because it is four-fifths of a mile long.

You hear the gasps from the people from Switzerland, Japan, the United Kingdom and everywhere else imaginable. People gaze skyward, point, stare, smile.

On the road here, you see their rented cars crawling up Highway 140 and Highway 120, or the young Europeans on their heavily laden bicycles, or oddities such as three motor homes in a row, going from scenic spot to scenic spot in a tight cluster.

Some wait their whole lives to witness this place for just a few days. Others come and stay. Yosemite Valley is full of people who call this place home. They are rangers, telephone repair workers, hotel managers, teachers. Theirs is a city, albeit an odd one, with a school, a church, routine and boring lives. There are also all the drifters, climbing bums, itinerant students, philosophers, outlaws and priests. None is ordinary. Studying their lives is not unlike turning over stones in the Merced River. You never know what you're going to find underneath.

ABOVE: A family's visit culminates with a swing in a red maple tree near the Yosemite Chapel.
OPPOSITE: The effects of wind, sun and a little time on the trunk of a high-country tree. The high country has remained unchanged for thousands of years.

The North American
Wall on El Capitan,
so-named because the
coloration in the granite
resembles the continent.
The first major ascent of
the face was in 1958,
and El Capitan now
challenges many
climbers each year.

ABOVE: A high-country cascade flows out of Rafferty Creek below Vogelsang High Sierra Camp.

RIGHT: Donna Karolchik of Santa Cruz finds a wooden throne next to the Merced River in Lower River Campground ideal for a late afternoon session of contemplation. "I was zoned out," she said.

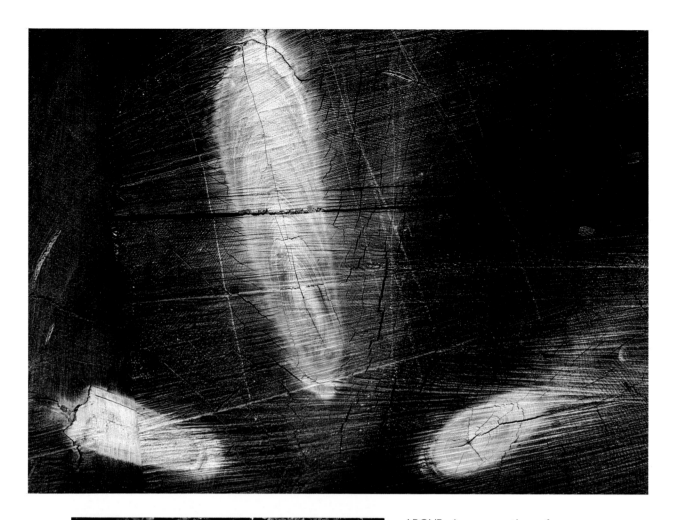

ABOVE: A cross-section of a tree in the Mariposa Grove of giant sequoias imparts beauty even while it decomposes.
LEFT: Before one can understand Yosemite, it is necessary to slow down and see the space between the leaves, says Tory Finley, a ranger who has adapted the words of writer Carlos Castaneda to the park.
OPPOSITE: Still growing after all these years, giant sequoias command the attention of Mike Carr, a Yosemite Institute instructor taking a break while members of his hiking group observe some of the world's tallest trees.

ABOVE: Los Angeles resident Danielle Gumbs sees snow for the first time in her life, expressing excitement and a victory smile—she had some difficulty walking across snow-covered bridges and hiking with snowshoes.
LEFT: Students from Watts in Los Angeles use sight, smell and touch to experience the park. Marisa Mares was surprised to discover the aroma of cinnamon in the bark of a Jeffrey pine, and found the sinewy texture differed from the bark of other species of trees nearby.

Swimmers in the Merced River above
Vernal Fall lie on the Silver Apron, a
glaciated slab of granite known for its slick
ride into a pool in the river. It's also known
to park rangers as a recurring location for
drownings during the summer.

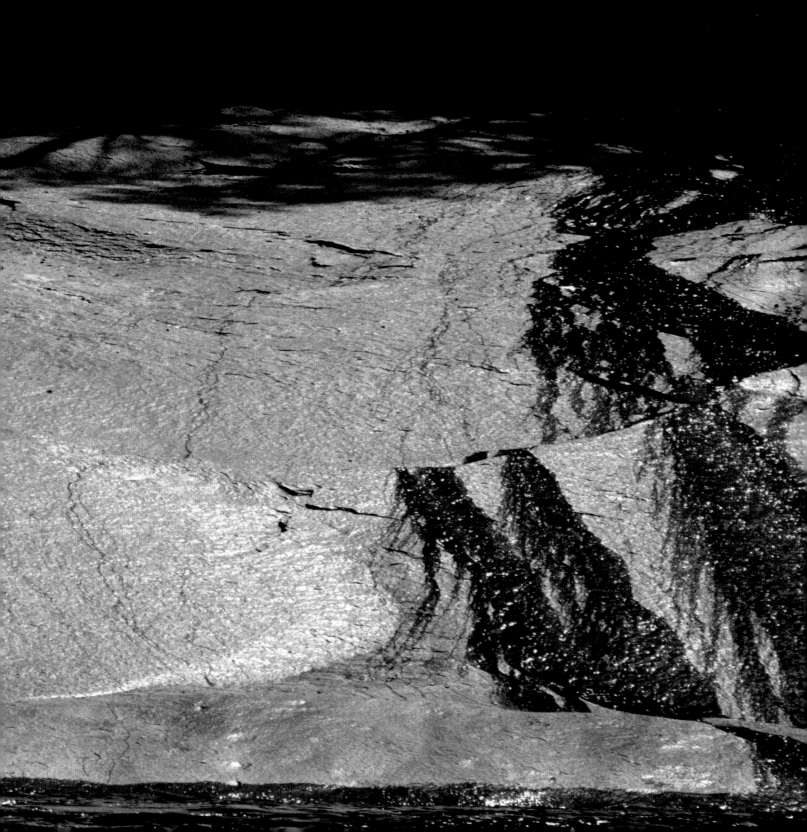

Campfire and sunset combine for aesthetics and warmth at the summit of El Capitan for Troy Johnson, a climbing veteran in the park. He has scaled the 3,000-foot face more than 20 times.

THE YOSEMITE EXPERIENCE

When Oliver Lippincott drove a locomobile over rough horse trails and entered Yosemite Valley in 1900, he was not only one of about 8,000 visitors, but the first ever to bring an automobile into the park.

He unwittingly started a trend. By the end of the century, more than 3 million visitors a year would pass through, a large number in cars.

As with any group counted by the millions, these visitors seem like a faceless mass to a casual observer, difficult to characterize. They jump out of their cars, crane their necks looking up, point, click cameras, park in the middle of roads (rangers say people check their brains at the gate), eat hot dogs, get sunburned, leave.

As a fellow visitor, you compete with them for hotel or campground reservations even before you set foot in Yosemite; after arriving, you wait in line with them at restaurants or bump into them on trails.

For some, such as Dan Clark of Cameron Park, a suburb of Sacramento, the competition comes as a surprise.

The first hint that Clark is befuddled is watching his car circle around the Lower River Campground on a warm summer night in Yosemite Valley.

The campground is full. Clark finally pulls into an undesignated spot and decides to take his chances with the rangers in the morning. Kids pour out of his car and set up camp.

Clark, 32, has not visited Yosemite since he was 12.

"It's funny how the park has changed," he says. He'd assumed it was the same. He didn't know the campground was booked solid through October.

"On a Friday, all my dad had to do was leave at noon, and there'd be plenty of space," says Clark. "California was plenty big enough. I guess more people are getting out.

"You used to see tents, and now everyone has a Winnebago. Just look at this," he says, pointing to a sea of metal trailers. "When we came, we had a '57 Ford station wagon. We had a trailer behind it. And we had one of those old green army tents."

Clark explains he brought his two children down to find what he experienced as a child. He asks whether the firefall still exists. The firefall was created when the coals of a large fire at the top of Glacier Point were pushed over the edge, tumbling hundreds of feet in a shower of sparks. It was institutionalized as a nighttime show by David Curry, owner of the camp concession, at the turn of the century.

"You'd see it shower off . . . it looked like Yosemite Falls," says Clark. "The whole time it was happening, you heard all kinds of 'ohs.' It was pretty incredible."

When told it no longer happens, he sighs. It ended in 1968, because it was not good for the environment. "I guess the whole world has become more environmentally aware," says Clark. "But without the firefall, it won't seem as special." He adds his kids don't know what they'll be missing, so it probably isn't a bad thing.

Yosemite has been changing ever since the first visitors arrived. Numbers shot up in 1907, when a railroad was completed up the Merced River canyon. The first 100,000-visitor year came in 1922; the first year a half million people came to the park was reached in 1940; the first million year was 1954; 2 million in 1967; and 3 million was reached in 1987. The next milestone, 4 million, seems an inevitable prospect.

How many visitors are too many? Endless argument surrounds this question. Conservationists are alarmed. Some old-timers dismiss the concerns. There's plenty of room, they say.

While crowding has some demonstrated ill effects, from a visitor's point of view, things are better than they used to be, even in the days when Clark visited as a child.

"Back then, the campgrounds and traffic were worse," says Jim Snyder, the park historian. "The campgrounds weren't laid out. It looked like the shelters after the earthquake in San Francisco. Now, fewer people can stay in the campgrounds, but it's a better experience."

But Snyder echoes the fear that the day may come when you will need a pass just to enter the park.

"The park is getting too popular now," agrees Tom Mack, a California native now living in Washington, D.C. He is sitting at the edge of a meadow in the high country, at a trail crossroads peppered with backpackers. "It wasn't this crowded 12 years ago."

Of course, crowds can still be utterly avoided—if you're willing to work for it. Some visitors go to great lengths—they ski over the back of the mountains in the dead of winter. One snowy day up in the ski hut at Tuolumne Meadows, we found a surprised Roy Lambertson, a Palo Alto resident who skied in with his friend Mark Fery of Spokane, Washington.

"You're the first mammals we've seen in four days, much less humans," says Lambertson. "We've seen tracks of animals, but that's it. Compare this to the summer, when 27,000 cars a day go down this road."

The two men are sun-reddened and tired, yet they strap on skis and head out in the last of the evening sun, traveling up a hill in snow that had fallen during a storm the night before.

They pretend to have downhill skis, shooting down the powdery hillside. The sky is now clear, deep blue, and the moon has emerged early. The hurrying sun drops below a peak, so only the tops of the granite domes catch the final alpenglow; Cathedral Peak is orange. Some ice slides off Lembert Dome, and all heads turn to see what this means. And when they turn back to the west, the sun is gone.

"Sure is purdy," says Fery.

Shadows deepen as they ski back to the hut across the frozen Tuolumne River. No further words are spoken.

But you don't have to strap on skis and brave avalanches and pain to enjoy the magnificence of Yosemite, even if in the middle of a crowd. Many months later, far down that river in the lower country, Cliston Taylor, 63, from Seminole, Florida is rendered just as speechless. He is one of several dozen tourists standing amid the Tuolumne Grove of big trees, ancient sequoias that range from 800 to 2,000 years old. He shakes his head.

"Can you believe how big that tree is?" he asks. "What's the diameter of the tree? Ten feet?"

He is told no. At least 18. "I'm going to go lay down next to it and have my wife take my picture, just to show how big it is." He hands her a video camera and flattens himself against the ground.

It's their first visit to California, and Yosemite.

"When I was a kid, maybe 10 or 12, a friend of mine and his family took a trip out to California. When they came back, he told me how they drove through a tree. He says it was in Yosemite."

He beams. He'd just driven through the tree.

"I've been waiting 51 years to drive through that tree."

Their first time in Yosemite, German hikers Martin Klupsch and Andrea Schulenburg enjoy the warmth of the morning sun at Sunrise High Sierra Camp.

Kim Orr, a member of the park's trail crew, begins a day by snugging her laces. Her boyfriend and trail crew member Dave McDonnell finishes a chapter in a book before leaving Little Yosemite Valley to go to the back side of Half Dome, where they will install the cables that will assist thousands of summer hikers to the summit.

A visitor can find any Yosemite he or she wants.
There is the Yosemite of crowds.
And there is the Yosemite of silence.

ABOVE: A lone hiker in Long Meadow, near the Sunrise High Sierra Camp.
OPPOSITE: With some 700 miles of hiking trails in Yosemite, a map is a good idea.
This hiker is on a trail above Vernal Falls, one of the most heavily used footpaths.

ABOVE: A visitor takes a break to battle mosquitoes on a horseback ride up the John Muir Trail.

BELOW: Ascending the narrowest passage along the Mist Trail near Vernal Falls, a group of hikers makes cautious progress.

OPPOSITE: A pair of hikers approach the rocky overhang on Half Dome for a stomach–churning view of the valley below.

"Mr. El Cap," alias Mike Corbett, begins his 42nd ascent of El Capitan. Corbett has climbed the world's largest granite monolith more than anyone in history and estimates that he has spent more than six months on the wall. While many observers think it is dangerous, Corbett says he finds peace while living in the vertical world of the mountain.

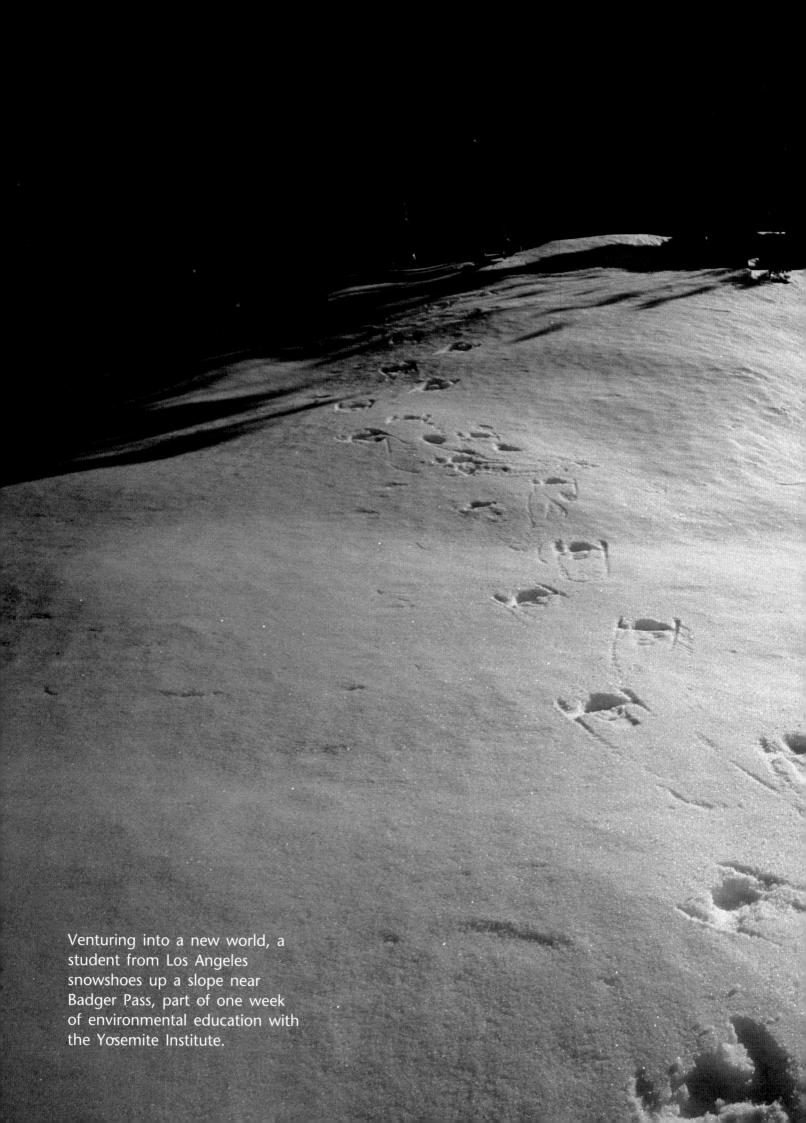

Venturing into a new world, a
student from Los Angeles
snowshoes up a slope near
Badger Pass, part of one week
of environmental education with
the Yosemite Institute.

ABOVE: Pre-flight checks are mandatory for hang glider pilots who take the 15 minute ride to the valley floor from Glacier Point. Roger Lockwood, the soaring ranger, checks out each glider's expertise before permitting the flight. RIGHT: Given the go-ahead, a hang glider takes off in the direction of Half Dome, as Lockwood ducks to avoid catching the wing tip. The controversial flights were suspended in the summer of 1990.

Next to Yosemite Valley, Tuolumne Meadows is one of the best-known parts of the park. In the winter, visitors must use cross country skis to reach the meadows, but in summer, thousands of cars travel the Tioga Road. Five-year-old Jaime Badia came with his parents, who were picnicking nearby. The Los Angeles youth found the low waters of the Tuolumne River an ideal playground.

> "*It taught me how to relax. To really relax.*"
>
> — Heidi Robison
> tells why she works summers
> for the Curry Company

ABOVE: The icy water in a pool at the base of Lower Yosemite Falls is tempting on a hot summer day.

LEFT: The spray of a waterfall peppers two seasonal Curry Company employees on an afternoon break from the Yosemite Lodge cafeteria. During the late summer, water in the falls is reduced to a near trickle. Other times, the thundering cascade is too dangerous to approach.

Many couples choose Yosemite for their weddings. Anders and Nancy Hedqvist of San Jose, Calif. came to the summit of Sentinel Dome above Yosemite Valley to get married.

In the spirit of Ansel Adams, a photographer using a large-format camera waits for the optimum light to record the beauty of winter from the Gates of the Valley observation area.

LIVING IN PARADISE

It is one of the few national parks with a self-contained community within its borders. By nature, it has to be different.

In the fall, as the pace of falling oak leaves quickens, there is a corresponding decrease in the number of visitors to Yosemite Valley.

When the branches of the black oaks are finally bare and stand stark against the cold granite walls, it becomes the time for the people who call this place home—those who make the park work—the grocery store workers, trail builders, rangers and others.

They breathe a sigh. They collect and talk. They stand out.

Their presence is something most summer visitors are not aware of, something some conservationists resent. Like it or not, the reality is that the residents are as much a part of the local flora and fauna as the trees.

While Yosemite National Park comprises 1,190.25 square miles, the most populous part of the park is the three square miles of Yosemite Valley between Curry and Yosemite Villages, where in summer, the population swells on some peak holiday weekends to more than 20,000. Come winter, there are only about 1,000 permanent residents.

If you're looking for residents and going highbrow, they can be seen drinking at the bar of the timeless Ahwahnee Hotel, which seems unchanged from 1962, the year John F. Kennedy strode in. Or you can go to the Mountain Room, the working-class bar.

But most likely, the residents are sitting at home, with the tube on, at least those who own televisions—a fair number do not. There are only two or three restaurants in the off season, two bars, one supermarket. There's no movie theater, no city hall. What services do exist close early.

You can't really call it a city, or even a town. It is one of the few national parks with a self-contained community within its borders. By nature, it has to be different.

It's a bifurcated community, a two-company town. On one side are the 600 or so employees of the National Park Service; on the other, the 1,800 peak season workers of the Yosemite Park and Curry Co., which has the contract to run most visitor services. They do not mingle much. In fact, resentment between the two communities has grown in recent years, because of friction over perceived differences.

In this mishmash of humanity, there is no mayor, but there are community leaders and citizens who fill the roles of life found in cities that have more normal boundaries and reasons for existence. There is a post office, a church, stores and workers who make the park run. There are even bums. Well, not real bums, but from the standpoint of social order, the climbers who live in tents at "Camp 4" are at the bottom. They hang around Degnan's Deli, drinking their beers and talking about the latest equipment.

Some of these people are running away from things. But others are running to something, which is an entirely different matter. Together, they make up the human face of the park.

THE CHILDREN

When Marni Grossgold conducts horse tours of the Yosemite Valley, she delights in leading tourists past Yosemite Elementary School.

"I take them behind here and point and say there's the school," says Grossgold, 29. "People say, 'There's a school here!' They can't believe people live here."

It looks like any other elementary school, except that its northern windows look out on Yosemite Falls plummeting 2,425 feet over a cliff. It has 81 students, and grades are mixed between four teachers. When the eighth-graders graduate, they attend high school in Mariposa, an hour away by bus.

This morning, the flag has been raised and there's normal childhood banter in the halls: girls self-conscious and trying to look pretty, boys bragging and awkward. Among a group of small children, one boasts that he turned 7 today. The ones who aren't yet 7 act jealous.

Catherine Soria, 39, begins her day with the second and third grades. Hers is the largest class. She has been teaching here for two years. Her husband is the park dentist.

All eyes are on her—no children gaze out the window at the dramatic cliffs that have become routine in their lives.

While the kids are working on math problems, she explains, "We came here for 11 years and never knew what was here. We never came through this neighborhood."

Yosemite Elementary School kindergarten students await their teacher at the beginning of the day. Visitors are surprised to learn there is a school in the valley that has more than 80 children through eighth grade.

When Soria and her husband discovered the community, however, they fell in love. "We couldn't resist coming here," she says. They gave up owning a home down in the Central Valley, and now they rent and live a totally different life. Soria finds it a better place to teach. It's a special place for education, she says, because there is a lot of parental involvement.

"There's a core group of 20-25 parents," says Soria. "You wouldn't get that in a school of several hundred kids in the Valley. I see there's an interest in the school that's almost extreme in a way. Parents want to know day by day what's going on."

This lifestyle, however, can be a trap, she says.

"It's rarefied. You feel your life is more special, or connected." She has to work against that. "But a lot of people here like the separation. They don't want to be culturally mixed. It's very different up here because there's no cultural mix, except for a few Indian students. I miss that."

As for the lack of diversity, she doesn't blame racism: "I think it's isolation."

Besides educating the young, the school provides an additional role as a place where those who work for the Yosemite Park and Curry Co. actually talk with those who work for the government.

"It's a centralized place for a meeting of people," says Soria. "If you are Park Service or Curry, there are very few functions that occur elsewhere that involve both. It's the only common meeting ground."

Regarding the division between Curry and park staff, "People in general are pretty careful about that—just like they wouldn't talk religion and politics," she says. "The issue is so volatile that it just doesn't come up. My husband and I love it because we're neither one. We don't have to take a side."

THE SINGLE MOTHER

Amy Ronay grew up in a resort environment—Aspen, Colorado—and her mother was a resort worker. Her father skipped out when she was young.

"He was never there, and I learned to get by on my own," says Ronay.

Her mother came to work for the Yosemite Park and Curry Co. in 1981. When Ronay was old enough, she joined the Curry Co. and adopted the resort worker lifestyle—being employed for nine or so months, and then roaming the world. She has gone everywhere, mostly Europe.

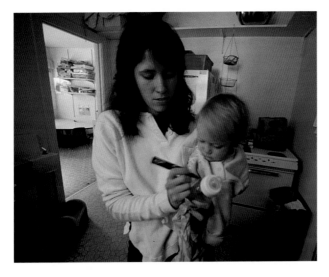

Amy Ronay says being a single mother in Yosemite is both rewarding and difficult.

Three years ago, she met a climber when she was in Germany. He later came to climb at Yosemite for a few days, and she wound up pregnant. She's never seen him since, and he doesn't know he's the father of Annika, just over a year old.

"So what?" says Ronay, 23. "He wouldn't do anything anyway." She says she got used to growing up with no father, so it is a normal situation.

Ronay is one of a number of single parents who call Yosemite home. Her daily routine is to drop Annika off at the crowded day-care center near Yosemite Elementary School and come to work as an assistant manager at the Yosemite Village Store.

Ronay has all the problems single parents face everywhere, but there are added difficulties: She is in desperate need of housing. There is little to be had for families in Yosemite Valley, and she is on a waiting list.

In the meantime, she lives with her mother in a trailer without running water below El Portal and commutes via the Merced Canyon more than a dozen miles each way.

"If you look at my car, half the time it's full of laundry or has mail stacked in it," says Ronay. She is lucky to have enrolled Annika in the day-care center, which now has a waiting list.

For Ronay, an obvious option would be to go to the city. "I lived in Fresno for a couple of months," she says. "I couldn't take it."

She fiercely clings to her life here.

"I want my daughter to grow up here. I would have wanted to grow up here. I want her to go to the school here. It's very good. When I lived in Fresno, I didn't know who my neighbors were. Here I know. A lot of people feel like protecting you.

"Working here, you get to know every piece of dirt about everybody, that so-and-so is cheating on somebody. You learn to live in a fishbowl."

That sounds like a downside, but Ronay says it has its advantages, especially working in the food store. "I know the guys who buy a six pack every day, or how many packs of cigarettes they buy. I know their bad habits and know who I don't want to date."

Most who come here are like her—they enjoy skiing or hiking. For those who don't, "These are the ones drinking the beer and watching TV," she says. "Yosemite Park caters to 'handicapped' people who can't make it anywhere else. They come up here and everything is taken care of for them—food, entertainment, and all they have to do is function and not do anything else. It's a good place to run to."

THE BASKET WEAVER

Of all the people who call Yosemite home, Julia Parker represents those with the highest claim to that statement—the Native Americans.

You can see her day after day in the little museum next to the visitor center, weaving a basket. She sits patiently and usually listens to the recorded voices of frogs and night insects.

Visitors shuffle through and watch. For more than 25 years, she has worked for the Park Service, showing and talking about the culture of the Miwok-Paiute Indians who used to live in Yosemite Valley.

Before Europeans came, there were an estimated 350 Native Americans living in Yosemite Valley. It's believed the first ones arrived 4,000 years ago.

By the 1930s, they were reduced to a roadside attraction. "A cute papoose is a real asset," gushed a 1931 account in the Yosemite Trip Book. "Many is the dime or quarter that travelers drop into the palms of Yosemite Indian squaws for the privilege of taking snapshots of the papooses." The cultural erosion increased after World War II.

"We don't have many of us living in the park," says Parker. "Just under 12. There was a small population when I came here in 1949. There were 75 people. They had an Indian village in one end of the valley."

For Parker, the passage of her culture has been a huge loss to Yosemite National Park. It is her job to retain as much of it as she can.

Parker is a Pomo and her husband, Ralph, who works as a supervisor on the road maintenance crew, is a full-blooded Miwok-Paiute. She keeps alive the Miwok tradition of basketry, and she tries to teach it to young people.

Basket weaving is an ancient and exacting craft. She often spends 200 hours on one big basket. She collects the willow shoots and other plants she uses for the baskets.

"We make people aware that we have cultural differences between us. We tell them the land gives us things, and like when we gather acorns, we say please to the tree when we gather. It's an important message to give the park visitor. We have to take care of the land. That's what this park is all about. It's our park. Or it was our park.

"You can't say, 'This is my land, get out,'" she says. "You have to accept the changes being made in the park. Even with the thousands of people that come in this valley, I still feel like it's the old times when I'm weaving a basket out there under a tree."

THE MINISTER

Ron Creque knows about running. The journey that led him to Yosemite began innocently enough when he was born 42 years ago in Huntsville, Alabama.

His father was an executive with a major corporation, and he grew up in a world where achievement was critical.

"From an early age you were taught to be successful and do the kind of things that would make you successful," he says. "There's a lot of drive in our family."

His first job was in management for a screw products company in Jacksonville, Florida. He rose to manager of a division of the GM Industrial Corp. Then, in 1972, his father, with whom he was very close, died suddenly at the age of 46 from a heart attack.

"It caused me to stop and ask what life is all about. My father, he worked and worked. He was always saying, one day, I'm going to do this, and I'm going to do that. I like the quote from Machiavelli that says we spend so much time

Julia Parker demonstrates the nearly lost art of basket weaving, practiced by her Native American ancestors. Visitors learn from Parker how reeds and twigs were gathered by the Indians—who roamed this land undisturbed for centuries before the arrival of Europeans.

getting ready to live that we never live. What is really important? I sold the house and headed to the seminary."

Now he's the interdenominational minister of Yosemite. Three other national parks have full-time ministers—Yellowstone, Grand Canyon and Sequoia-Kings Canyon. His church is the oldest valley building, erected in 1879.

Creque sits in its office, looking out at the hoarfrost-covered ground. He ran here, he says, and succeeded in changing his life.

"You've got a lot of people who are coming to something," he says. "And we have a percentage who are running away. Yosemite is a good place to hide, and at certain times of the year, you can just show up and get a job. It's a good place to get their lives back together. Broken relationships and bad parents or even criminal activities are in the background of a lot of people."

But many fail to find what they hoped for.

"Problems tend to get magnified, and people think about them more. Some people come here who aren't into backpacking, and there's not a whole lot for them to do. This place can be real lonely for the single people. There are a lot of alcohol problems. They get in a pattern of sitting in front of the tube drinking every night. It's a rut for some. It's a real paradox when you think about it."

THE CURRY WORKERS

Glenn VanWinkle was halfway through his senior year at California Polytechnic State University, working at a part-time welding job.

One day something happened.

"I came out of the factory and looked east and said, 'What am I doing here?'" That was it. He quit everything and drove east to Yosemite with his girlfriend. Both hired on with the Yosemite Park and Curry Co.

He started as a maid. "The first few days, I said to myself, 'What am I doing here?'" The girlfriend left. He stayed and stopped asking those kinds of questions. That was 1983.

No longer a maid, he has risen through the ranks of the Curry Co., as the park concessionaire is simply known. The company's roots date to 1899, when David and Jennie "Mother" Curry came and set up some tents at the base of Glacier Point. Curry is now part of the Hollywood-based MCA Corp. and a veritable industry in the park. Curry employs roughly 600 permanent workers and an additional 1,200 seasonal workers.

In the right season, it's easy to get a Curry job—it's not unlike joining the Foreign Legion or some expatriate community. Some have used the job as a steppingstone to other pursuits—former Curry employees include actor Robert Redford, environmentalist David Brower and the late photographer Ansel Adams.

There are many jobs: in the valley hotels, the restaurants, the ski area. Among the most coveted are the 40 seasonal positions in the six high-country wilderness camps.

Each camp is a day's walk from the other and is open only during the two-month summer season. Tourists come on mules or hike in. By city standards, the camps are crude. They consist of tents slung over concrete slabs, with iron beds. But in the setting of remoteness, the camps are truly castles. Mule trains pack up steaks, salads and other items of luxury one can only dream about when roaming a trail. There are even hot showers.

The Sunrise High Sierra Camp, which VanWinkle runs, is at the edge of Long Meadow, at 9,300 feet, where the cool air feels like fall even in summer. The jutting hulk of Half Dome rises to the south, visible from a knoll behind

Those who live in Yosemite are charged with helping preserve it for future generations, as are the thousands of visitors.

OPPOSITE: Andrea Goodman, a Curry Company summer employee, tends to the task of cleaning the restroom facilities at Sunrise High Sierra Camp. Six such camps spaced a day's hike apart allow many park visitors to see the back country without the usual burden of a fully loaded backpack.

camp, and it reminds us that Yosemite Valley is not all that distant. But it would take two days of walking to get there.

It's clear and the sky is sharp. Music fills the air, and it comes from VanWinkle's tent. He's playing a guitar and looking out his flap at the city of tents scattered amid the pines.

Six people work for him in this camp, and they serve the 34 tourists who sleep here each night. VanWinkle, 28, and the cook are permanent Curry employees, and the rest are college students, busy with evening chores. It's dark when they finish and begin playing poker.

They gather at a table in the kitchen beneath the harsh glow of gas lanterns and divvy up match sticks in lieu of chips.

Cards fly back and forth. They play games such as baseball, 727, stud and guts. On their powerful tape deck, fueled by a large battery pack, is new-age music of the Windham Hill label.

"What we need now is some ice cream," laments Heidi Robison, 23, a senior English major at the University of California, Davis. Ice cream is one of the few commodities unavailable here.

VanWinkle is the oldest face at the table. There is a lot of banter and name calling, but the truism about poker revealing the nature of people applies, and it is clear these are very decent people. Even if the boss is winning big. VanWinkle finally loses a hand, and says, "Look, my pile of sticks is going down," and the workers groan, because he has a veritable forest of matches in front of him.

The group has been up here for more than a month and has grown quite close. Robison says she's left only once, and that was to hike out and drive to Sacramento to see the Grateful Dead. She regrets it. She says it broke the spell that is this place.

The evening ends with VanWinkle the clear victor. It's the first time he's won in weeks. The group retires.

Few of them sleep in the tent cabins provided. Instead, they roll their sleeping bags out on the granite slabs under the stars, having come to a consensus that the tents are uncool and off-limits. They merely throw their bags on the rocks and get bitten by the mosquitoes. They have grown oblivious to their bites.

"We just get a lot of welts," says Sidho Ganghdharan, a New Jersey native and pre-med student at Dartmouth College in New Hampshire.

Each day begins at 6 a.m., and each day, a new crop of guests rotates through. Meals must be cooked, beds made, wood cut, things cleaned.

Chores rotate, and it's Robison's and Ganghdharan's week for cleaning the tents. Robison wrestles with a sheet.

"I've been a camp counselor, in food service, worked at a computer company—but for a summer job, this is by far the best I've had," she says. Last year, she taught English in Taiwan.

She adds, "I really want ice cream now!"

Ganghdharan, who smooths a sheet, drove out from New Hampshire just for the interview on the chance that he might work up here. "I'm going to do the Peace Corps for two years," says Ganghdharan, who has one year of school left. "I came here to think what I want to do."

While they continue to make beds, camp worker George Lamore, a senior at the University of California, Davis, has the morning off, and he slings a rope, carabiners and climbing nuts over his shoulder and strikes out to practice climb above camp.

We scramble up the granite slabs to a high point and Lamore picks a route. He heaves himself up over a rough spot and sits looking out at the world. Lamore, whose father worked for an oil company, grew up in Indonesia. He came seeking something and he thinks he has found it. What he can't understand are some of the tourists.

"There's two kinds of people up here," he says. "There are those who appreciate the work it takes to get up here. And there are others who miss the point of the whole place. One lady said, 'If I was at the Hilton,' and I couldn't believe it. To mention the Hilton and this place in the same breath!"

"There's two kinds of people up here. . . There are those who appreciate the work it takes to get up here. And there are others who miss the point of the whole place."

— George Lamore,
camp worker

"Take a look around you," he adds, and his hands arc past Long Meadow, Bug Dome, Vogelsang Peak and the distant peaks of the Clark Range. Shadows from fast-moving cumulus clouds race across the meadow far below, and we can see horse packers working their way along.

We pick our way back to camp and watch the cowboys in their black hats who bring dudes and food up here; they sit in the shade, spitting and looking cool; a backpacker buys a hot shower for two bucks; the workers prepare for the dinner rush.

They serve 39 meals tonight—roast lean pork, fresh bread, salad, home-made soup, corn, apple cobbler and potatoes. They find time to play Frisbee out in the meadow in the light of the sunset alpenglow. They clean up, and again play poker. VanWinkle loses a lot of his matches. They laugh, go to bed too late, get up early, and do it all over again.

Many months after the season in the Sierra ended, Robison is back at school in Davis. She finally got her ice cream. But now she's missing something she'd found in a meadow high in Yosemite National Park.

"If anything, one thing it did for me was it taught me how to relax," she says, and then she pauses, thinking this sounds like a cliche. "To really relax," she adds with emphasis, trying to explain the unexplainable. "Not just physi-cally. It was such a wonderful, non-cerebral thing."

THE POSTMASTER

You could call him an old-timer, but nothing about Leroy "Rusty" Rust, the postmaster of Yosemite, is old.

Yet it seems he has been here forever. He was born in Yosemite in 1920, and his father was here long before that. There's a picture over Rust's desk of his father driving a stagecoach up a dirt road carrying tourists into the valley in 1907. The family's association with the park dates even further back. His grandfather came just after the park was founded in 1890 and helped build the high country trails.

The only significant period of time Rust has been away from Yosemite was during World War II and his college days.

The old ones who founded the

Postmaster Leroy "Rusty" Rust was appointed by John F. Kennedy in 1963. The post office is a focal point in the Yosemite community—there is no home delivery, so just about everyone comes by during the course of a day.

park were not a humorous bunch, he says. "I knew Mother Curry. She was a tough lady. Good stock. All the pioneers were. My grandfather . . . I was scared to death of him. He was a big, tough old guy."

You usually find Rust darting around the Yosemite post office, a grand old building with an oak lobby, built in the days when the government spent money on design as well as mere function.

Rust's office probably doesn't look much different from how it did on the day in 1963 when President John F. Kennedy signed the appointment naming him postmaster. A portrait of JFK hangs on the wall, and Rust is proud of that. He met Kennedy when the president came to the park a year earlier.

A sign proclaims that the office has gone since 1952 without an accident. "And I was the accident," says Rust of that day. A rope broke on a mail sack and he dislocated his knee.

All roads lead to the post office. Beginning about 11 a.m., and through the course of the day, the community filters in to check the boxes—there is no home delivery here. Because of this, Rust is one of the more visible members of the village. He is respected and sought out for things that need doing.

He is a past president and current member of the Lions Club—he rues the day someone else started a Rotary Club here, and says the small community needs it "like a cowboy needs hemorrhoids."

Skiing is his life. It has become legend in the park that he once skied off of Glacier Point down an alarmingly steep chute that plunges almost straight for 3,000 feet into the valley—roughly the same place hang gliders jump off from today.

Rust has seen a lot of change in his time here. He points to the picture of his father driving the team of horses through billowing dust. "He hated the dust. He thought blacktop was the best thing invented."

That seems to epitomize Rust's view of change. The "golden era" of the park was "when I was 18. I keep telling the kids it's all downhill after that."

The park, he says, "is still nice. You can still get away from people very easily."

THE LAWMAN

There was once a passionate kid from the San Fernando Valley who loved the outdoors.

He was the son of a Bavarian mountaineer and a mother who was an artist from Amsterdam. At age 5, his parents took him on his first camping trip, and that was to Yosemite National Park.

The boy disdained team sports, preferring instead to hike and rock climb. At age 14, he joined a Boy Scout Explorer post. They didn't have any uniforms or any of "that nonsense." What they did have was a leader who further solidified his love of the wilderness. It was an intense love, and the young man knew his Holy Grail—and that was to become a ranger.

He wanted to be the very best. A good ranger helps people. A good ranger helps nature. He followed these virtues with his characteristic intensity; all of his work brought him to Yosemite and his dream.

And so, 14 years after he began his quest to be the best ranger ever, ranger Kim Aufhauser is sitting in the living room of his home in Yosemite Village, listening to a Vivaldi piccolo concerto, and his eyes are sagging, tired after a long shift.

The wood stove is hot. There is no television in this home. It's a hated object. But there are many books. His wife, Lisa Strong-Aufhauser, sitting next to him, met him when he was teaching a class in cardiopulmonary resuscitation. He feigned fainting, and she goofed up, letting his head fall to the floor. After that, "it was love at first thump," he says.

Now, at the age of 33, it is as if Aufhauser is a character in a Guy de Maupassant story who has suddenly come to a cruel realization.

"The things I wanted to become when I became a ranger haven't happened," Aufhauser says with a sigh. "I spend less and less time doing ranger work. Maybe my expectations were too high. Maybe I had a holy notion of wrestling bears, enjoying nature. But then the reality check set in."

The reality is that rangering has evolved more and more into straight police work and less of helping nature and people. Morale has sunk. "I think morale is bad top to bottom, left to right," says Aufhauser.

Park Superintendent Michael Finley admits it is a huge problem—and it's not unique to Yosemite. There is less money for parks. There are ubiquitous politics. And society has changed. More urban problems are coming here—drug dealing, occasional homicides, endless domestic disputes, embezzlement.

"Sure, it isn't as bad as East L.A., but it has gotten worse. The park visitor has changed," says Aufhauser.

In the old days, rangers simply had to don a Smokey Bear hat and work. They didn't even have guns. In contrast, Aufhauser is a full-fledged medic, a deputy coroner, a firefighter, a technical rescue expert. Plus, he's in charge of the weapons program. He's had teeth cracked by a man in a seizure and guns pulled on him. He's climbed icy cliffs in horrible weather to rescue climbers. For all of this, his base pay is $21,000 a year.

Officers with the California Highway Patrol, who don't have to be medics, firefighters, cliff climbers or coroners, earn a base pay of almost $39,000 a year at the end of four years.

"My father makes $100,000 a year. He's worked hard for it. . .But I want something different."

— **Kevin Fleming, member of the Yosemite trail crew**

"It's less to me the poor salary than I'm doing less and less of what I want to do," says Aufhauser. "We are losing touch with why we are here. We're losing touch with nature."

In the end, however, "I love the Park Service," says Aufhauser, who can't imagine himself in a more conventional job. "The thought of looking at somebody's teeth all day or writing up wills—I couldn't do that."

THE TRAIL BUILDER

Some are drawn to the endless sea. Others to church. Still others to the desert.

Kevin Fleming finds his truth in rock.

Fleming, 26, a New Jersey native, is a member of the 40-person trail crew at Yosemite. His job is to break up stone and build walls, stairs and trails.

Today, he is working on a project at Happy Isles, at the far end of the Yosemite Valley where the road ends and the wilderness starts. Fleming is part of a crew of seven constructing a trail for disabled visitors.

It's complex work. Two crew members are at the top of a hill, enveloped in dust as they power 80-pound star drills into granite to cut it. They sling the blocks on cables several hundred feet down to Fleming, where he unloads it. Other masons set the stone in the wall they're building. No cement is used. Except for the gas drills, it is centuries-old technology.

Fleming wipes his beard and awaits a load of rock—it weighs 150 pounds per cubic foot—to be winched down. He unstraps a 200-pound stone.

"The thing about the trail crew is the people doing this kind of work don't do it for money or achievements," says Fleming. "You have to like hard work and stone work."

He explains that the work is a reward unto itself.

"A lot of people who hike by look at this with disdain. A schoolteacher who came by said breaking rocks is tough and he shook his head. I said, 'What do you do?' 'I teach,' he said, and he said it was easier than breaking rocks. That's debatable."

Fleming pitches rocks into a pile and explains that Pulitzer Prize-winning beat poet Gary Snyder worked the trail crew here and was inspired to write such works as "Rip Rap and Cold Mountain Poems."

"My father makes $100,000 a year. He's worked hard for it, and deserves it after all the years he worked for it. But I want something different."

This job is a tool to understand, he says.

The Merced River is high and rushing, and the trees thick here on the Happy Isles. Fleming, who has been doing this for five summers, looks around, waiting for the sun to break over the valley rim and warm things up. In the winter, he goes to college. He is a religious studies major and hopes for a degree by the time he is 30.

"I want to get myself into the lifestyle I like, away from the city—get into a creative living situation, a creative working situation. By no means am I a hermit. But the world is much too hectic and caught up in itself."

The workers look satisfied with the wall that is slowly going up. It is a mosaic of beautifully interlocked and perfectly cut stone. They figure and rub chins as to what will come next, which rocks will have to be moved.

"And you did all that before noon," one says proudly.

Members of the Park Service trail crew perform the annual ritual of installing cables on the backside of Half Dome, which allow hikers to gain the summit safely. The cables are placed before Memorial Day and taken down after Labor Day to keep winter weather from destroying them.

THE THREATENED LEGACY

A lingering frost covers the field. A large buck grazes nearby. The animal is unconcerned as a group of children and park biologists walk into the meadow south of the Yosemite Elementary School and begin a long process that will require ultimate patience—the planting of a grove of oak trees.

Oaks have been vanishing in Yosemite Valley. The reasons are complex. When whites came, the fires that periodically cleared out the pine trees were controlled. Pines, which crowd out oaks, have been slowly taking over ever since.

Further, the deer population has skyrocketed, partly because visitors feed them, and any oaks that manage to sprout are quickly eaten by the ravenous animals. And with many hundreds of thousands of people coming to the valley, they are also trampled by the blitzkrieg of so many feet.

People in Yosemite are a never-ending source of controversy. Some say there are too many visitors. Others argue a visitor can find any Yosemite he or she wants. There is the Yosemite of crowds. And there is the Yosemite of silence. It doesn't take long to walk away from the road and find yourself alone, even in bustling Yosemite Valley.

While this is true, people do have an impact—the oaks are but one example of the flora and fauna that have been altered by the presence of humans.

In a program that is the first of its kind, biologists devised a way to reverse the decline of oaks by planting 700 native black oaks on the eve of the park's centennial year, involving the elementary school's 81 students.

A group of second-and third-grade students listen while biologist Ben Alexander explains this process.

Alexander asks the children how fast do they think the trees will grow. They shake their heads while looking at trees not much taller than a finger.

"You will grow faster than the trees," he answers. It won't be until they are 18 or so that the trees will surpass them in size.

The children work with adults and start planting. Yosemite Falls provides a backdrop. Alexander contemplates that in a half century, these children will be able to come back and see a tall grove of mighty oaks where now only a damaged meadow exists.

From an aesthetic point of view, it's tragic the oaks have been vanishing. But more than aesthetics are at stake: The trees are critical for the survival of wildlife, says revegetation specialist Richard Hadley. Some 20 species of birds utilize the oaks, as well as owls, squirrels, and other animals. A stand of pines offers little for these creatures. Pines are a biological desert compared to an oak grove or a meadow. There used to be 600 acres of meadows in the valley 100 years ago, and now there are 400.

"Meadowland and oak woodlands are incredibly diverse ecosystems as opposed to a conifer forest," says Hadley.

A lot of work went into planning the restoration project. "We planted some acorns but they were browsed down," says Hadley. Undaunted, the biologists devised mesh screens to line the holes to keep out root-eating squirrels, and a special mesh cover for each sapling to ward off deer such as the nearby buck.

As the kids plant, many visitors here on holiday stop by and offer to help. "That's something that happens regularly on a 'reveg' project," says Alexander. "They want to do something for the park. Last year in the Tuolumne revegetation, a German who was just walking by stayed three days."

In the Tuolumne Meadows project, the park closed off portions of meadows crisscrossed with trails and planted 50 different species of native grasses and plants.

But it is Yosemite Valley that gets most visitors. The impact visitors have had here has been extreme.

"Over the last ten years there's been a noticeable increase in trails cutting across the meadows and the loss of riparian habitat," says Hadley. "People are roaming off the existing trails that aren't adequate for the current level of use. It isn't like the city where things are fertilized and irrigated. Natural vegetation is very fragile."

Human activities outside the park also affect Yosemite's flora. While many European weeds and grasses came when whites started farming in Yosemite Valley, other exotics have taken longer to arrive. It was in 1987 that biologists first noted star thistle in the park, after years of slow migration up from the Central Valley. Every star thistle plant means some native plant used by wildlife is crowded out.

"Hand pulling is the only successful method of eradicating it," says Hadley. They have been weeding and experimenting with controlled burns.

El Capitan times two—commercialism in the park is a continuing controversy, as is the debate over the impact of several million annual visitors.

Human activity also seriously affects not only the plants, but the park's wildlife.

Steve Thompson is part of a two-person wildlife biologist team at Yosemite. They are vastly understaffed and unable to do much original research. It all stems from a lack of money. Thompson outlined what is happening with some species and what they have been trying to do with limited resources.

BEARS

The bears at Yosemite have become geniuses.

It used to be you could foil them. In the old days, you could put your food in a tree and that would keep them away. But they educated themselves.

First, if you threw it up over a branch, counterbalancing it with a sack of rocks, they learned to tug on the rocks until the food bag dipped close enough to the ground. Then some bears learned to chew through branches. If the branch was too thick to gnaw, they figured out how to climb trees and leap through the air, grabbing food sacks in midflight.

"They're getting smarter," declares Thompson. "We used to advise people to sleep away from their food. Now we're thinking of advising people to sleep near their food. If you give them long enough, they'll get any food."

The effect has been that bears now are found in the high country where they never before existed, because there naturally was not enough food.

PEREGRINE FALCONS

Only a few pairs of peregrines are known to nest in all the Sierra, and most are in the park.

"As long as DDT is used anywhere on the globe, we're going to have a problem," says Thompson. "The birds winter in Latin America, and they bring it back with them."

DDT turns into chemical DDE that thins the shells, dooming reproduction. Unknown, he says, is the effect of organic pesticides used in the Central Valley that may or may not turn into DDE in the birds. "There needs to be more research to confirm the source of that," he says.

The birds exist by the grace of human intervention. Sometimes, the park takes eggs from some nests and incubates them—otherwise, the bird's weight could crush the thin, poisoned shells.

MOUNTAIN SHEEP

They vanished from the park around the turn of the century. In 1986, the park reintroduced a herd of 27 wild Sierra bighorns in an area of Lee Vining Canyon on the east slope of the Sierra.

The original sheep were killed off by hunting and diseases introduced by domestic sheep.

When famed naturalist John Muir was pushing to make Yosemite a national park, he was bitterly opposed to domestic sheep grazing in the high country meadows. He called them "hoofed locusts" because they stripped meadows.

Domestic sheep are gone, but they still affect the park and this new herd of their wild cousins. Biologists fear if now-unused sheep grazing areas near the park are ever reactivated, the domestic sheep could introduce diseases to the wild sheep that would doom them. Wild sheep cannot adapt to these diseases.

"They need a buffer from tame sheep to survive," says Thompson.

FISH

"We have a wish list, and certainly a natural salmon run would be great," Thompson says of the salmon that used to run in the Merced River. "The hurdles we'd have to go through are rather large—some big dams between here and the ocean."

But aside from the vanished salmon, the Merced River "is not the same," says Thompson. "A lot of changes have occurred to its shore. Because we have rafting, we have to keep snags out of the river. Those snags provide ideal fish habitat. The river is wider because of erosion. The reason there is erosion is the vegetation is stripped along a lot of the shore by foot traffic. The bridges have also created a scouring effect downsteam from them."

YELLOW-LEGGED FROG

"We deal with the evident species but we don't have an idea about the less glamorous species. We don't have a handle on the yellow-legged frog. They've been vanishing all over the Sierra. Some people have pegged it to acid rain. They're an indicator species. If something is wrong with them, it will affect other species."

Other problems?

"Bird watchers anecdotally are seeing a decline in song birds," says Thompson. "What we're seeing occurring is the effect of what's going on in tropical rain forests. I think the park has great scientific value because it's a relatively untouched ecosystem to monitor these things. It's all related to the number of people who come here. That's our main problem, trying to mitigate these impacts."

A question is put to him: What if an additional one million people were to come to the park each year? He sighs and considers this as he might ponder a potential murder spree.

Rafting on the Merced River seems environmentally benign, but experts say that clearing the river of logs and debris for the boaters has harmed fish habitat.

Even before the Indians, many creatures called Yosemite home. Some animals have had difficulty adapting to the growing intrusion of people, but others have found ways to survive and even thrive. Next to one of the busiest roads in the valley, these mule deer cross the Merced River .

A city on wheels waits at the Arch Rock entrance on Highway 140 at the beginning of a Memorial Day weekend. As many as 20,000 people can be found in Yosemite Valley some holidays.

*How many visitors
are too many?
Endless argument
surrounds
this question.*

ABOVE: Yearning to escape the steel jungle of a traffic jam, a young girl strains for her first glimpse of the valley.
LEFT: The Yosemite Park and Curry Company operates an open-air tour of Yosemite Valley.

Youthful visitors pack themselves along walkways on the Stoneman Bridge over the Merced River and watch the dangerous leap into the pool below. This activity results in dozens of injuries each year.

ABOVE: A riverside bush becomes a makeshift drying rack for soggy clothes.

BELOW: The only swatch of "green grass" in Lower River Campground was left by visitors who forgot to pack their synthetic carpet.

OPPOSITE: In the lazy days of summer, campfires throughout the valley's campgrounds add a bit of pollution to the park experience. Increasing pollution from the smoke and a lack of firewood have prompted park officials to consider banning campfires.

ABOVE: George Lamore, a Curry summer employee at the Sunrise High Sierra Camp in the Yosemite backcountry, smashes cans so they can be more easily carried out by mules. LEFT: Trouble brews regularly during the busy summer months for valley rangers such as Kim Aufhauser, kneeling. Aufhauser and Curry Company security personnel investigate what turned out to be the work of a maurading bear that tore apart a Curry employee's tent.

Streaking into the night, a car
exits the Wawona Tunnel
above Yosemite Valley, dubbed
the "Whiskey Tunnel" because
it's four-fifths of a mile long.

Fire and water:
While rangers now have to set
controlled burns to restore the natural
balance, other forces of nature are
beyond any manipulation.

ABOVE: Breaking the silence of winter, snowplows work along the Tioga Road from Crane Flat to the eastern park boundary at Tioga Pass, the highest crossing in the Sierra at 9,941 feet. Mountain residents eagerly await the road's opening come spring—it signals the return of tourists and dollars to the local economy.
RIGHT: The spring runoff is in full swing where the Merced River plummets over Vernal Fall, on its way to California's Central Valley.
OPPOSITE: Fire management is a subject of controversy, especially after the 1988 Yellowstone National Park fires that quickly raged out of control. A "let-burn" policy usually prevails when Yosemite fires begin naturally. This blaze, however, along the Tioga Road, was eventually doused by firefighters.

ABOVE: After nearly a century, bighorn sheep were reintroduced to Yosemite in 1986. The bighorns here are being moved to the park from a herd near Bishop, California. A sheep is airlifted to waiting trucks for shipment to Yosemite.

RIGHT: Wild sheep were decimated by hunters and disease from domestic sheep that once grazed in the park. Several years after the move, the sheep seem to be thriving around Lee Vining Canyon on the east side of Tioga Pass.

Oaks have been vanishing in Yosemite Valley.
The planting of young oaks symbolizes
the hope for restoring the natural balance.

ABOVE: The lack of wildfires is partially to blame for the disappearance of black oaks in Yosemite Valley, which need fires to clear out competing pine trees. In an effort to ensure that oaks survive, biologists decided to plant them by hand; the netting placed around the oak seedlings shines in the afternoon light. The netting was used to protect the small trees from deer, for which the saplings are a delicacy.
OPPOSITE: Yosemite Elementary School students Sara Saunders, left, and Robin Meely help park biologists plant seedlings in a meadow next to the school playground.

Watchful students from the Yosemite Institute meet a hopeful mule deer looking for a handout. Park policy is to discourage humans from offering even so much as an outstretched hand. The policy is aimed at reconditioning the animals to seek their natural food supply.

STEWARDS OF THE PARK

A visitor to Yosemite might assume that those wearing ubiquitous Smokey Bear hats are all simply rangers, lumped together in a group, each with the same purpose and goals.

While they look alike, the duties of Yosemite's rangers vary widely. The only bad weather many rangers experience is the blizzard of paper work atop their desks. But for some rangers, such as Carl Sharsmith, it means looking for little things and telling people about them.

The 87-year-old ranger spends his summers in Tuolumne Meadows, (opposite) explaining grasses and flowers—such as penstemon, columbine, Yosemite aster and Mariposa lilies—to visitors.

For other rangers, such as Brent Finley (above) work means being the guardian of the High Sierra during the long, bitter winters.

Others do things that inspire everyone: Ranger Mark Wellman left his regular duties at the visitor center, got out of his wheelchair and climbed El Capitan.

In the following pages are the stories of special rangers. But no matter what roles the scores of rangers perform, they all share a common purpose: protecting Yosemite.

THE NATURALIST

"*Progress can go in either direction.*"

— Carl Sharsmith,
ranger

The golden age of the park is a matter of speculation and interpretation. People over 40 view the 1950s with nostalgia. Those a little older speak of the 1940s.

For Carl Sharsmith, 87, the best time in the park was immediately following 1930, when he started working as a ranger-naturalist in Tuolumne Meadows. For Sharsmith, it was a golden time because the country was so wild.

"It ended when they put that boulevard up there," he says of the modern paved Tioga Road that was improved and dedicated in 1961. "It was part of the old wagon road. That is what kept it so pure. Progress can go in either direction."

In spite of the change, he still loves Tuolumne, the largest subalpine meadow in the Sierra Nevada. He lives in a tent there each summer and has grown to legendary status for the nature walks he gives. "I have covered every square inch of that country time and time again. I have been eager to baptize everybody in the Yosemite flood," he says.

In the winter, he is found at California State University, San Jose, working hard at mounting dried plant specimens. He started that job in 1950, and built most of the collection of 15,000 plants on file.

The park was just 40 years old when he started working in Tuolumne Meadows. By then, there was little sign of the sheepmen or miners left from 1890, when the park was founded.

Now, 60 years later, Sharsmith says he realizes how little 40 or 60 years really are in terms of that fragile high country.

"They forget that recovery is slow," he says of the marks of humans in the meadows. "And with increasing altitude, it is even slower. In Tuolumne, you have to talk in terms of 50 to 100 years."

As an example of how slowly things heal, visitors can still plainly see the "T" blazes carved on lodgepole pines by the U.S. Cavalry around the turn of the century, to mark trails. Some look less than a few years old.

Sharsmith has a love affair with the fragile little high country plants. His favorite? "I think I'll vote for the pigmy daisy. I rave about that little fellow. It's 3 inches tall. You have to be up by timberline to see it. There is a charm about these things."

Sharsmith worries about the future of Yosemite. There have been all sorts of proposals over the years to do things in Tuolumne—such as downhill ski slopes. He has little faith that more ideas won't be drummed up.

"Tuolumne is not safe. It's a good thing the public is aware." For the future, he fears that visitors may have to be limited. "There's going to have to be rationing. That's all. It can't take much more."

Carl Sharsmith, the venerable ranger-naturalist of Tuolumne Meadows, is one of the foremost authorities on Sierra vegetation.

After an autumn snowfall, Sharsmith and his group hike along a trail that follows the Tuolumne River. Many visitors relish walking with the famed high-country naturalist. While everyone notices the obvious sights in the park, Sharsmith is known for showing visitors the little things that often go unnoticed.

ABOVE: Sharsmith's stories are now legendary, attracting hundreds of people every summer who listen to the oft-told tales. Old friends like Ann Matteson, who lives near Yosemite, enjoy his monologues.
LEFT: The 87-year-old ranger delights in telling humorous stories of his life.

"My walk
is all the
entertainment
I need."

— Carl Sharsmith

ABOVE: Sharsmith's tabletop has his biography and pipes spread on a bandanna. RIGHT: Sharsmith leads a Spartan life in his tent near Tuolumne Meadows, where he spends his time reading the plays of Shakespeare, reviewing his own writing and relaxing with his pipe. He takes a regular evening walk to his beloved Tuolomne Meadows. "When you know all these things it is easy to be entertained. My walk is all the entertainment I need."

Corbett was 35, looking for a new challenge . . . Wellman, 29, was looking for some way to go beyond his wheelchair. They were a perfect match.

In the world of rock climbing, Yosemite put the United States on the map. It was here that big wall climbing came into its own and most of the great strides in the sport were made.

The golden age began in 1958, when Warren Harding, George Whitmore and Wayne Merry made the first major ascent of the 3,000-foot granite face of El Capitan. Dozens of climbing firsts followed. All the big names were here: Royal Robbins, Chuck Pratt, Yvon Chouinard. These men were the Academy Award winners of rock climbing circles, and Yosemite was their Hollywood.

The most renowned of these climbs happened in 1970, when Harding and Dean Caldwell attempted El Capitan's "Wall of Early Morning Light." They quickly ran into trouble—big trouble—but refused to be rescued. The climb ended an amazing 27 days after it started, with more than 75 newspeople waiting at the top.

But those glory days ended. All the firsts were completed. Ascents became a routine thing for tourists to stop and watch from the meadow next to the El Capitan straightaway at the base of the cliff.

When Mark Wellman came to Yosemite in 1986 to be a ranger, he looked at El Capitan and the granite face awed him, perhaps not unlike the way it awed the first men who climbed it. But any hope of climbing it seemed a faint dream—he was wheelchair-bound.

Wellman didn't know then that he would run into veteran climber Mike Corbett.

In late 1988, the two men got to talking, and they decided they could make it up as a team. If they did it, Wellman would become the first paraplegic to climb El Capitan. It sounded crazy. But Wellman thought about it, and the desire to leave his wheelchair behind and go up the rock burned in him.

Perhaps he desired to overcome the mountain because it was a mountain that had put him in a wheelchair — he was scrambling on Seven Gables Peak south of Yosemite in 1982 when he fell more than 100 feet. He spent a night wedged in a crack before being rescued, and the spinal injury left his legs mostly paralyzed.

Corbett had different motives. Corbett was lured to Yosemite on the heels of the climbing greats. He'd come to Yosemite after high school, hungry to take it all in. He moved into a tent, working odd jobs to support his climbing habit. His first time up El Capitan was in August 1977. By the spring of 1989, he'd spent a lot of hours on the wall, having been up that rock 41 times—the world's record for ascents. "Some of my finest hours have been on El Cap," he says.

Corbett was 35, looking for a new challenge—a climbing first in a world where it seemed all the firsts were done. Wellman, 29, was looking for some way to go beyond his wheelchair. They were a perfect match.

But from idea to reality was grueling work. Special equipment, such as pants to protect Wellman's legs, had to be designed. Wellman, who already had a massive upper body from weight lifting, took his training into high gear. He would literally pull

Mark Wellman at work as an interpreter and information ranger in the Valley Visitor Center. He was injured in a climbing accident.

himself up the mountain on a device hooked to the rope, and he would have to be strong.

And there was danger. The rare accidents that do happen are usually among Europeans, unfamiliar with American conditions. Rescue rangers say that if you look carefully at the base of the big walls, you can find human bone shards—bodies explode when they fall for hundreds of feet, and it's impossible to gather all the pieces.

But the men were confident. They did 35 practice climbs. On July 19, 1989, they were ready. Corbett carried Wellman piggyback to the base of the wall and they started climbing.

Wellman was intensely focused on the climb, and did not welcome all the publicity. He declined elaborate comment. "I want to wait until I get to the top to blow my horn," was all he would say.

Eight days later, when they made the summit, there were 50 waiting newspeople and cheers from mobs of tourists down in the valley. The climb put Corbett in league with the greats of his youth. For Wellman, it proved that paraplegics can do things.

And it was a lesson in teamwork.

Something else happened out of the climb that might never have occurred—something that touches on the fact that so many people in Yosemite are running to or from something.

In the middle of the climb, with the feat being broadcast nationwide on the nightly news, Corbett's family finally discovered where he had been all the missing years. Corbett hadn't told anyone in the media that he hadn't seen his mother in 20 years and his father in 15. When he reached the top, a network satellite linked them up.

Corbett never explained why he was estranged from his family, saying only that some "stuff" had happened.

He later downplayed any sense that he'd come to Yosemite to escape.

But he did say, "You realize there's nothing out there for you after a while. You go down in the city and it's tough. It's an easy life up here. You don't see anyone busting ass up here. Well, maybe the maids and food service people, the trail crew. It's like watching the world happen but being removed from it."

Wellman didn't blow his horn at the summit. He was his usual quiet self.

"I don't know how to say this, but I do what I do . . . and it seems to be a bigger deal to other people," said Wellman. "I've been out of a wheelchair now for eight days. I haven't been out of a wheelchair for that long since my accident." He added that a paraplegic can do almost anything. "If you feel you can go for it, do it."

ABOVE: The first daylight touches the summit of El Capitan, the world's largest granite monolith. The 3,000 foot vertical face is a world-class challenge to rock climbers.

OPPOSITE: Mark Wellman, a Yosemite Valley ranger-interpreter, prepares for his assault on El Capitan. Wellman trained for six months for the climb.

Mike Corbett, top, and Mark Wellman scale the last few hundred feet of the Shield Route on El Capitan. Wellman became the first paraplegic to climb the wall. After a mountaineering accident in 1983, Wellman lost the use of his legs. His spirit endured. The week-long climb was the longest he had been out of his wheelchair since the accident.

"*Some of my finest hours have been on El Cap.*"

— Mike Corbett, climber

RIGHT: Weary but triumphant, climber Mike Corbett helps Mark Wellman up to the summit of Yosemite's El Capitan on the final day of their historic but grueling climb. At the start, they had to haul 200 pounds of water and gear behind them. "I'm tired," Wellman said at the end. "I have pains where I didn't even know I had parts."

OPPOSITE: Mark Wellman winces from pain and fatigue. To scale the wall, he literally performed 7,000 pull-ups. While the climb will go down in the record books, it was also a classic story of a team working together. "We had a system going," Wellman said. "You have to have so much trust." Climbers in general capture the spirit of freedom in the park, and months after the climb, Wellman in particular was still being sought out by tourists at the visitor center where he works to talk about the feat.

"My appreciation for this place grows. A lot of people would really like to have this kind of life."

— Tory Finley, ranger

It isn't easy to pay a visit to Brent and Tory Finley.

You pull up behind their pickup truck and face their driveway—all 12 miles of it. Then you must put on cross-country skis and a pack and start trudging.

The Finleys are winter rangers, guardians of the eastern half of Yosemite National Park. For the six or so months that trans-Sierra Highway 120 is closed, this ranger-couple lives snowbound at 9,000 feet, isolated in an Alpine world of rock and ice. In modern America, it's hard to get more than 10 miles from a road. The Finleys may be among the most isolated couples in the lower 48 states. Because of park rules that forbid machines, the Finleys do not jet around their domain on snowmobiles. They must use cross-country skis, as do any visitors.

When you leave the cars behind and step from the dry pavement into the blinding snow, you begin a trek toward one answer of what Yosemite National Park means.

Cross-country skiing is work. Nothing exists in your mind but the ascent ahead. Lungs heave in the thin air and you push uphill through Lee Vining Canyon toward Tioga Pass. The trail is the snow-covered road, but that belies its difficulty.

For those unfamiliar with Nordic skiing, you go uphill by essentially sliding the skis along and pushing with two poles. Progress is slow in the mush—it's bad snow. It is only several hours before dark when the 10,000-foot pass is reached; the wind is howling through the gap, and storm clouds are stacking. Eight miles remain to be traveled.

There are coyote tracks and scat, purple with juniper berries. It has been a starvation winter for the coyotes, for the scat contains only these berries, eaten in desperation. You wonder what they think as they range across this haunting country and its trails flanked by lodgepole pines.

Downhill is easier, but not much. It becomes mindless, repetitive work. The only thing you become aware of is the snow ahead, and those storm clouds. The major sound is the noise of skis breaking fast through the crusted snow as night falls. It is a curious sound, bearing an uncanny resemblance to human voices—expressions such as "Hey!" and "Look at that!" You answer your partner's questions and find he's been silent.

The lodgepole have their own voices, with the gentle assistance of the wind, softer and less distinct.

The journey transforms from a physical act to a mental conquest. Muscles long ago gave out. Still, you go on, certain you will not make it, and then you are there: it is dark, and the lights of the Finleys' cabin emerge from the forest, a warm yellow glow in the wilderness of white.

Brent, 32, is at the stove. Tory, 30, is on the phone. He is 6 feet tall, she much shorter. Both have angular bodies and raccoon eyes the shape and form of their sunglasses, the whiteness surrounded by deeply tanned faces from the reflected sun of days spent on snow.

"We eat a lot," says Tory. They burn it off working. "We call it the Finley fat and

fun factory," says Tory. "You eat all you want and don't get fat."

Eyes slowly become accustomed to the cabin's brightness. Even more slowly do you become aware of the surroundings. There are modern amenities—lights, a stove, a refrigerator, a phone and a television. It all seems so out of place.

There is, however, a wood stove that is their heat, and a full quarter of the living room devoted to skis and ski equipment, various waxes, waxing irons. Ten pairs of cross-country skis line a wall. Here, skis are like horses were in the Wild West—a matter of life and death.

This is their second winter in this cabin. The qualifications are to be married, be expert in emergency medical care, law enforcement, skiing, handiwork and perhaps most importantly, to be willing to be alone with your partner for half a year.

"I'll never forget that first year and everyone left and it was storming," says Tory. "It was real lonely. We came inside and popped a bottle of champagne. A lot of people don't have the partner who could stand it."

The previous winter, only 270 people came by their cabin in six months. But in the summer, on any given day, thousands of cars pass on the road before it closes. That's the difference a season makes.

It is part-time work—one of them is paid for four days, the other three—and it is only seasonal. They started working at Yosemite in 1984, as valley rangers, and they began wintering in Tuolumne in 1987. "I think my appreciation for this place grows," says Tory. "A lot of people would really like to have this kind of life."

As for Brent, he feels weird when he goes to the city. "I've become a bumpkin, I guess," he says. What he noticed most on a trip to Los Angeles was "people's faces. You forget how many different faces there are."

They both know they have a unique situation and they cherish it. They have a

Brent and Tory Finley, winter rangers in Tuolumne Meadows, live in isolation from the rest of the park. The high-country rangers are on patrol above Dana Meadows on the western side of the Sierra.

television, but they watch it only occasionally to keep up on news. "I prefer to read," says Tory.

The news is on now, and it confirms what their eyes and instruments have been telling them—a very large storm is going to hit tonight.

After dinner, they settle in with some hot tea. The conversation turns into a discussion on life and happiness. Tory faced the fast track. Both her parents are attorneys. Her brother is an attorney and her two sisters are teachers.

"It was real important that I achieve," she says. But she rejected that. For Brent, who grew up in Kansas, the decision for this life was more basic. "It sounded like fun," he said. "And it has been."

But for Tory, she says, "If you stop in our society, you realize the kind of life we live. I had to make a decision to slow down. I think this job made me realize I could slow down. And that I liked my life better when I slowed down. I do better with simplicity.

"Part of me is intrigued by the city," says Tory. "I miss movies. But when I go there I feel a sense of claustrophobia and I can't stand it. I went through a period of time when I was terrified to drive a car. I find it really hard to go away from this place."

There is more conversation along these lines. You realize that for them, the process of sorting life out is not an occasional pastime but a continuum, constantly defined and redefined.

Brent and Tory retire for the night. Sometime after midnight, the storm hits and 50 mph winds buffet the cabin. In the morning, they sit at their kitchen table, watching in awe.

"Snow, snow, snow," mutters Brent. "It's been snowing for six hours and we have nine inches. That's one-and-a-half inch an hour. That's pretty heavy."

About 10 minutes later, he looks out the window at the snow depth marker and exclaims, "Now it's snowing sideways! That was a good gust."

And so they wait for the snow to end. They indulge in eating a fresh pear brought up by the snow survey crew a week before. They cut it in half and savor each bite, taking 10 minutes to eat the fruit.

But then it's time to work. Their job varies with the season. In the fall, they patrol the park perimeter to keep poachers out. In the winter, they are there for any rescue work needed for the rare visitors who pass this way. They are police, poets, explorers, but today, they are scientists, testing the snow for avalanche danger and water content.

They pull skis off the rack, bundle up and kick across a field, throwing new powder, heading up a hill through a thick forest.

They find a steep slope. It is a complicated test, requiring a massive trench to be dug, and many readings to be made with gauges.

> *"I see the small things. I see the river opening up. I see a new crack in a wall to climb. . . If we stop, we can see the space between the leaves."*
>
> — Tory Finley, ranger

ABOVE: Brent and Tory Finley, the winter high-country rangers of Yosemite. LEFT: Brent Finley nibbles on a peanut butter sandwich while surveying a winter blizzard in progress outside the kitchen window.

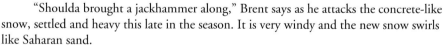

"Shoulda brought a jackhammer along," Brent says as he attacks the concrete-like snow, settled and heavy this late in the season. It is very windy and the new snow swirls like Saharan sand.

An hour or so passes as they work, and thick clouds muscle their way low and close to the mountain peaks. Now and then the sun pokes through.

"Many people come here and they are really affected," says Tory as Brent digs. "I don't know how many times I've gone down to the hut and people talk about all sorts of intimate things in their life," she says of the cabin provided by the park service for the cross-country skiers who pass through. "They come in and just gush."

But those who come through for a few days or a week are only at one level of experience, she feels. Society is like a huge machine that works on us, and it takes a long time to shut it off.

"It's like when we're standing on a mountain and there is a sunset—they see the whole thing," she says of visitors. "I see the small things. I see the river opening up. I see a new crack in a wall to climb. I think of Carlos Castaneda, in his book, 'Journey to Ixtlan.' He says if we stop, we can see the space between the leaves."

This, to her, is the meaning of this place.

Later that night, the wind has subsided and the wood stove is stoked. She pours some tea. To see the space between the leaves, she says, "it takes time to get there, to that really 'deep' place."

Television is more than a luxury for the Finleys; its weather reports are a vital tool. Part of their job is monitoring High Sierra weather conditions, including snow depth readings and avalanche conditions. The living room of their one-bedroom cabin also serves as a ski workshop and laundry room.

The Finleys view a winter sunset from the summit of Lembert Dome. Cathedral Peak with its pointed summit stands on the horizon.

THE FUTURE

Stewardship will carry a growing responsibility as millions more flock here.

In the beginning, back in the smoking abyss of time, there was molten rock. It would cool and become granite, lift skyward; an age of ice would come and go, and a few other things would happen over the course of several billion years in the earth's history.

Only then, in a fraction of a second in the scheme of all this, would a two-legged creature enter Yosemite.

No one is certain when the first Indians came. The arrival of whites, however, can be precisely measured—1851. Many detrimental things happened between that year and 1890, when Yosemite was made into a national park. Its preservation was supposedly assured, but in 1913, Congress authorized a dam at Hetch Hetchy on the Tuolumne River, drowning a nearly duplicate Yosemite Valley—and other mistakes were made regarding development in the park.

As the presence of modern men and women in Yosemite approaches the one-and-a-half century mark, the worst threats now appear to come from crowding and the ill effects of pollution.

The park has become not unlike an island, when viewed from a jetliner crossing the mountains at night from the east. All across the supposedly empty Nevada desert and the eastern slope of the Sierra are the indicators of people—in the form of sparkling lights. But when the Yosemite country is crossed, a delightful black void opens and it's almost possible to mark the park's boundaries by the lights that fringe it.

You know that dark place is wild country, wild only because society has deemed it remain so. It will become a more distinct island as California's population swells. Stewardship will carry a growing responsibility as millions more flock here to find a piece of the world as it once was.

And what a piece of the world it is.

Yosemite is a place of moments: the crisp tone of mountain light striking Half Dome before the sun dips and is lost over the coastal mountains to the west; the chatter of the Merced River on a winter day as it falls toward the ocean; a rainbow emerging from the mist of a waterfall; natural oddities like grass growing in the shape of a heart in a patch of gravel.

OPPOSITE: After a light winter storm, the face of El Capitan catches the first light of day.

At sunset, when it is quiet and lonely and a full moon shines down on the Merced River in Yosemite Valley, it is hard to believe more than 3 million visitors pass through this park each year.

Hugh McCann, a college student from Texas, stands at the brink of the valley rim at Taft Point after a late spring strorm, looking down on the clouds erupting from the abyss below.

A vigorous hike up Mist Trail from the Yosemite Valley floor turns into an unexpectedly colorful experience as a rainbow appears around Vernal Falls. The 2-mile trek up switchbacks attracts thousands of visitors each year.

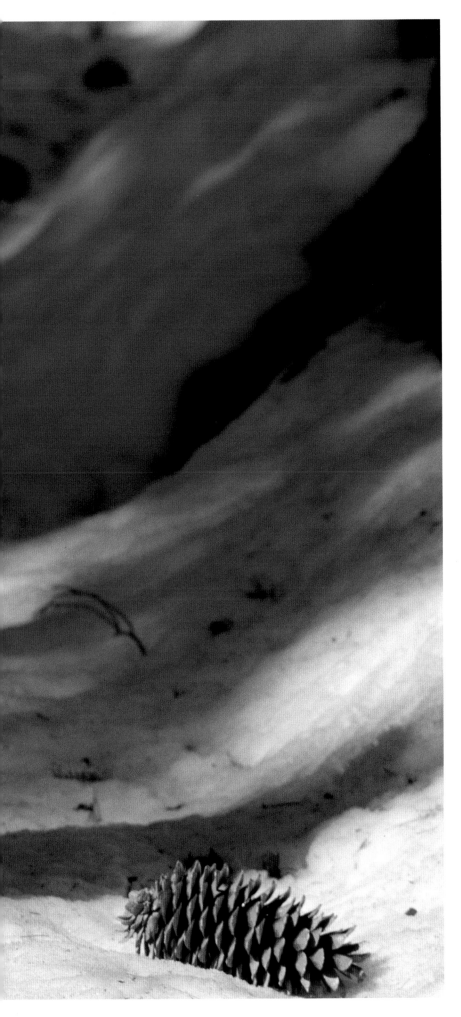

ABOVE: Hikers marvel at the ever-changing landscape created by swirling clouds on the rim of Yosemite Valley.

LEFT: As it has since its creation in 1890, Yosemite National Park offers people the opportunity to discover nature—and themselves. Dorothy Limbach, a Los Angeles resident participating in a program of environmental education for senior citizens, stops on a walking tour of the Mariposa Grove of giant sequoias to admire and photograph a sugar pine cone.

*The park has become not unlike
an island. . .it is wild country,
wild only because society
has deemed it remain so.*

LEFT: A jogger enjoys the sunlight of a late winter afternoon.
ABOVE: Tuft love—dwarf grasses grow in a heart shape in the alpine
environment above Boothe Lake.

ACKNOWLEDGEMENTS

Jay Mather is a photographer for *The Sacramento Bee*. He was a co-winner of the Pulitzer Prize for international reporting in 1980 while at *The Louisville Courier-Journal* for photographs of Cambodian refugees. He has won numerous other awards, including the Robert F. Kennedy journalism award.

Dale Maharidge is a *Bee* reporter. In 1990, he won the Pulitzer Prize in non-fiction for *And Their Children After Them*, a book he co-authored on Alabama sharecroppers. He also co-authored *Journey to Nowhere, The Saga of the New Underclass*, and has won numerous journalism awards. Both men have extensively hiked, climbed and rafted the American West.

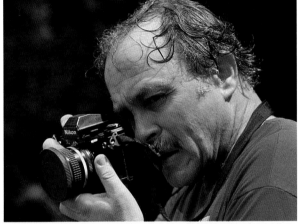

LEFT: Photographer Jay Mather at work in Yosemite.
BELOW: Writer Dale Maharidge during one of his trips to the park. The two spent two years gathering material for this book.

Photograph by Mark Morris

Book Design & Picture Editing
George Wedding

Editor
Terry Hennessy

Art Director
Howard Shintaku

SPECIAL THANKS TO:

In Yosemite
Steve Medley, President, The Yosemite Association
Mary Vocelka, The Yosemite Association
The Yosemite Institute
John Poimiroo, Yosemite Park and Curry Co.
Don Pitts, U.S. Magistrate
Kim Aufhauser and Lisa Strong-Aufhauser
Jim Snyder, historian
Roger Rudolph, chief ranger
Bob Johnson, Mather District ranger
Dennis Carlock, principal, Yosemite Elementary School
Brent and Tory Finley, rangers
Leroy "Rusty" Rust, postmaster
Lisa Dapprich, Mallory Smith & Marla LaCass,
Yosemite National Park public affairs office

And all people in Yosemite National Park who extended support.

The Sacramento Bee
Gregory Favre, executive editor
Peter Bhatia, managing editor
Ed Canale, assistant managing editor
Mort Saltzman, assistant managing editor
Tim Connors, publishing systems engineer/graphics
Dave Adams, color printing

Photograph by Jay Mather

Yosemite: A landscape of life was designed and edited using Apple Macintosh™ personal computers and SuperMac™ Technologies color monitors. Photographs were digitized for position purposes using a Nikon LS3500 scanner. Pages were designed with Aldus PageMaker™ software and output to a Linotronic L300R high-resolution imagesetter. The book is printed on 100 lb. Ikonolux book text paper, by DuMont Printing, Fresno, Calif. Color separations were done by FilmCraft, Inc., San Jose, Calif.